Journey to Athens

Grades 1–3

Table of Contents

Welcome to Athens 2	Olympic Logos 18
Making and Using the Mini-Books 3	Sports to Sort 22
Ancient Olympic Games Mini-Book 4	The Marathon 23
Modern Olympic Games Mini-Book 6	Track and Field Jeopardy 24
Host Cities 9	Top Athlete 25
U.S. Host Cities 10	Bend and Stretch 26
Map of Europe 11	United States Medal Winners 27
Olympic Spirit 12	Making a Mascot 28
Do Your Best 13	The Flag and Emblem 29
Play Fair 14	Medals 30
Olympic Village 15	The Torch Relay 31
Training Table 16	Bibliography 32
Venues 17	

©2004 by GRIFFIN PUBLISHING GROUP/UNITED STATES OLYMPIC COMMITTEE

Published by Griffin Publishing Group under license from the United States Olympic Committee. The use of Olympic-related marks and terminology is authorized by the United States Olympic Committee pursuant to Title *36 U.S. Code* Section 220506. U.S. Olympic Committee, One Olympic Plaza, Colorado Springs, CO 80909.

All rights reserved. No portion of this book may be reproduced in any form without written permission of Griffin Publishing Group and Teacher Created Materials.

10 9 8 7 6 5 4 3 2 1

ISBN   1-58000-120-3
TCM   3747

DIRECTOR OF OPERATIONS	Robin L. Howland
PROJECT MANAGER	Bryan K. Howland
WRITER	Cynthia Holzschuher, M.Ed.
EDITOR	Ellyn Siskind, M.A.
COVER DESIGNER	Brenda DiAntonis
ART MANAGER	Kevin Barnes
ART DIRECTOR	CJae Froshay
ILLUSTRATOR	Ken Tunell

Griffin Publishing Group
18022 Cowan, Suite 202
Irvine, CA 92614
www.griffinpublishing.com

Published in association with
and distributed by:
Teacher Created Materials
6421 Industry Way
Westminster, CA 92683
www.teachercreated.com

Manufactured in the United States of America

Welcome to Athens

Athens is the capital city of Greece. It has a rich history. Athens was the birthplace of the ancient Olympic Games and host to the first Modern Games in 1896. Now the city is ready for visitors from around the world to enjoy the 2004 Olympic Games.

Two new railways and an airport were built to make travel easy. New hotels are ready for people who will watch the Games. There is a new Olympic Village for athletes, and an ancient marble stadium has been restored for the opening and closing ceremonies.

What do the following words mean?

ancient: _____

_____

birthplace: _____

_____

stadium: _____

_____

ceremonies: _____

_____

restored: _____

_____

Finish this sentence:

I would like to go to the Olympic Games in Athens because _____

_____

_____

_____

_____

Making and Using the Mini-Books

Materials:
- copies of pages
- scissors
- glue
- stapler
- two precut 4" x 5" (10 cm x 12 ½ cm) sheets of construction paper (front and back covers) for each book

Procedure:
1. Distribute the pages and have students cut them apart.
2. Direct students to glue the cover page to one piece of construction paper.
3. Tell students to organize the book pages in sequential order with the front and back covers in place. Check the order and staple once in the top left hand corner.
4. Remind students to add their names to their front covers.
5. Allow time for the students to color the pictures.
6. Use the books for independent reading or in reading groups.

As a follow-up to the books, have the students cut out the vocabulary cards below and match them with the corresponding pages in their books.

boxing	discus	javelin	wrestling	weightlifting
fencing	cycling	running	jumping	sailing
horse races	pankration	marathon	swimming	gymnastics

Ancient Olympic Games Mini-Book

The Ancient Games

by

_____
(student's name)

1

Boxers wore special gloves. They fought until one gave up or fell down.

2

A man needed to be strong to throw a discus made of stone. The winner made the longest throw.

3

There were horse races and chariot races. Every rider wanted to have the fastest horse.

4

Ancient Olympic Games Mini-Book *(cont.)*

The javelin is a wooden spear. The athlete won by making the longest throw or hitting a target.

5

Pankration was the most dangerous of all the ancient games. It was part wrestling and part boxing.

6

Running and jumping are the oldest Olympic sports. All athletes needed great speed to win.

7

Wrestling was an important Olympic sport. The wrestler who threw his opponent down was the winner.

8

Modern Olympic Games Mini-Book

The
1896
Games

by

_____
(student's name)

1

Pierre de Coubertin was the founder of the modern Olympic Games. He hoped the games would promote friendship and fair play among athletes from around the world. 2

Running, jumping, and throwing contests took place on the first day.

3

Fencing and weightlifting contests were held on day two.

4

Modern Olympic Games Mini-Book *(cont.)*

Shooting, lawn tennis, and cycle races were held on day three.

5

All kinds of gymnastic contests took place on day four.

6

Wrestling matches and the marathon, a 26.2 mile race, were held on day five.

7

Swimming events were held on day six.

8

Modern Olympic Games Mini-Book *(cont.)*

The torch parade took place on day seven. After the parade, winners went to the palace for a banquet with the royal family.

9

Sailing events and cycle races were held on day eight.

10

Rain out! All events were canceled due to heavy rain.

11

The King of Greece gave athletes an Olympic Games Certificate, an olive branch, and their medals at the closing ceremonies.

12

 # Host Cities

The Olympic Games have been hosted by different nations all over the world. Being the host nation is a very difficult job. The host must provide places for the athletes to live, eat, practice, and compete. The host nation also welcomes millions of fans from around the world.

Here are just some of the challenges that might face a host country. Discuss the first question in each set below as a class. Then, answer the second question on your own on the lines provided.

1. There will be hundreds of different languages spoken. How will everyone understand one another?
    - How many languages other than English can you name? _____
    _____

2. Different cultures eat different types of food. How can you find out what different people eat, and how will you get the right food?
    - Do you know the names of any foods from other countries? _____
    _____

3. It may be difficult for some athletes to be so far away from home. They might get homesick. How would you make them feel more comfortable, more "at home"?
    - Have you ever been homesick? _____
    _____

You and your family may have been hosts at some time. Did you ever have friends or relatives as guests in your home? Did they stay overnight or longer in your home? In the box below, write a short paragraph about the experience and the ways in which you and your family were good hosts.

Welcome
Willkommen
Boa vinda
Recepción
Benvenuto
Välkomnande

 # U.S. Host Cities

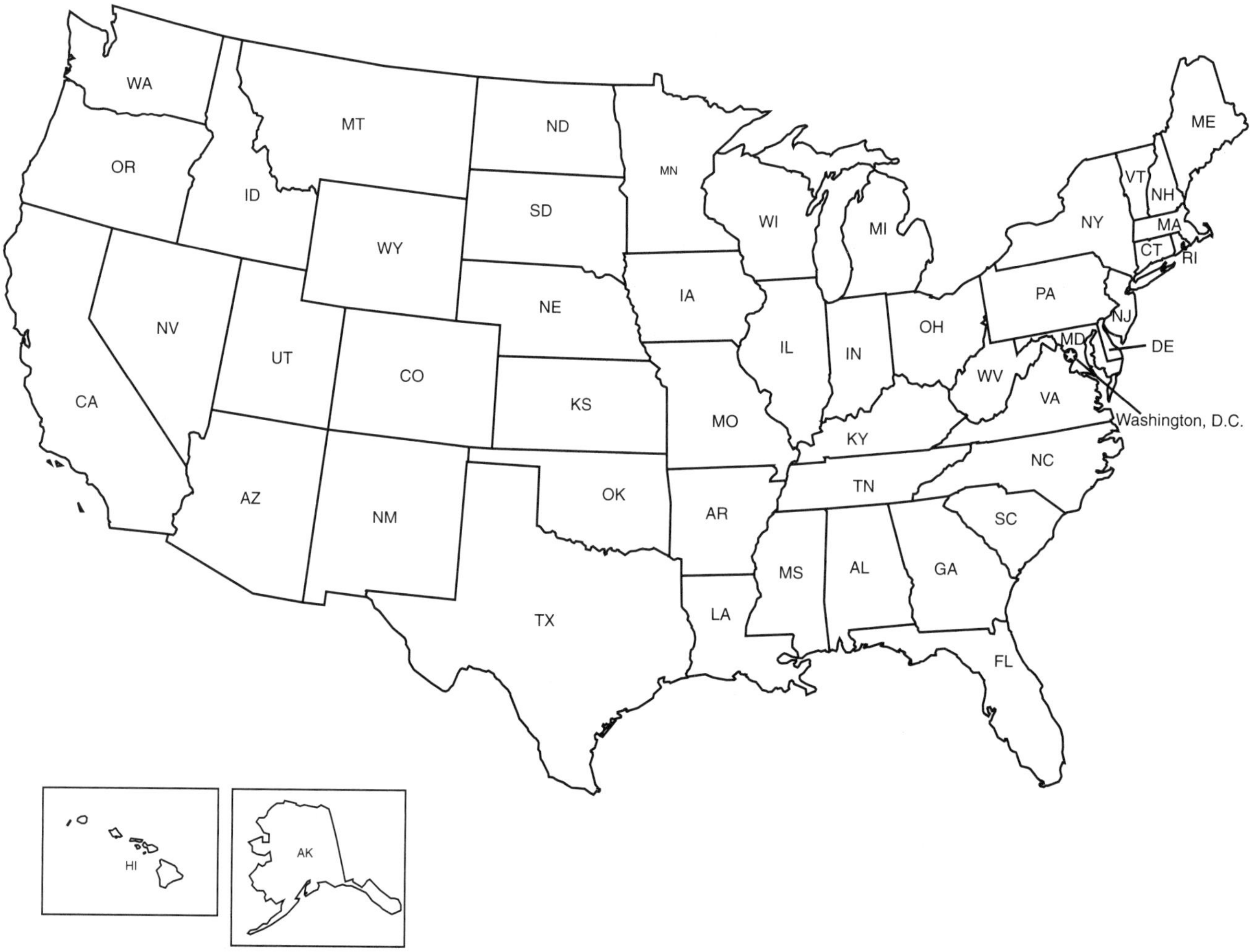

The United States has hosted the Olympic Games in six different locations. Find these states on the map and color them:

- St. Louis, MISSOURI
  (Summer, 1904)

- Lake Placid, NEW YORK
  (Winter, 1932, 1980)

- Atlanta, GEORGIA
  (Summer, 1996)

- Los Angeles, CALIFORNIA
  (Summer, 1932, 1984)

- Squaw Valley, CALIFORNIA
  (Winter, 1960)

- Salt Lake City, UTAH
  (Winter, 2002)

 # Map of Europe

Greece is one of many countries in Europe. This is a map of Greece and nearby countries. The capital of Greece is **Athens**, the site of the 2004 Olympic Games. It is marked with a star.

Looking at the map, complete the following activities:

1. Find **Greece**. Color it yellow.
2. There are four countries that border Greece.
   - Find **Albania** and color it red.
   - Find **Turkey** and color it green.
   - Find **Bulgaria** and color it orange.
   - Find **Macedonia** and color it purple.
3. Greece is surrounded on three sides by seas. Find the names of the three seas and write them on the lines below. Be careful to spell them correctly!

_____

_____

_____

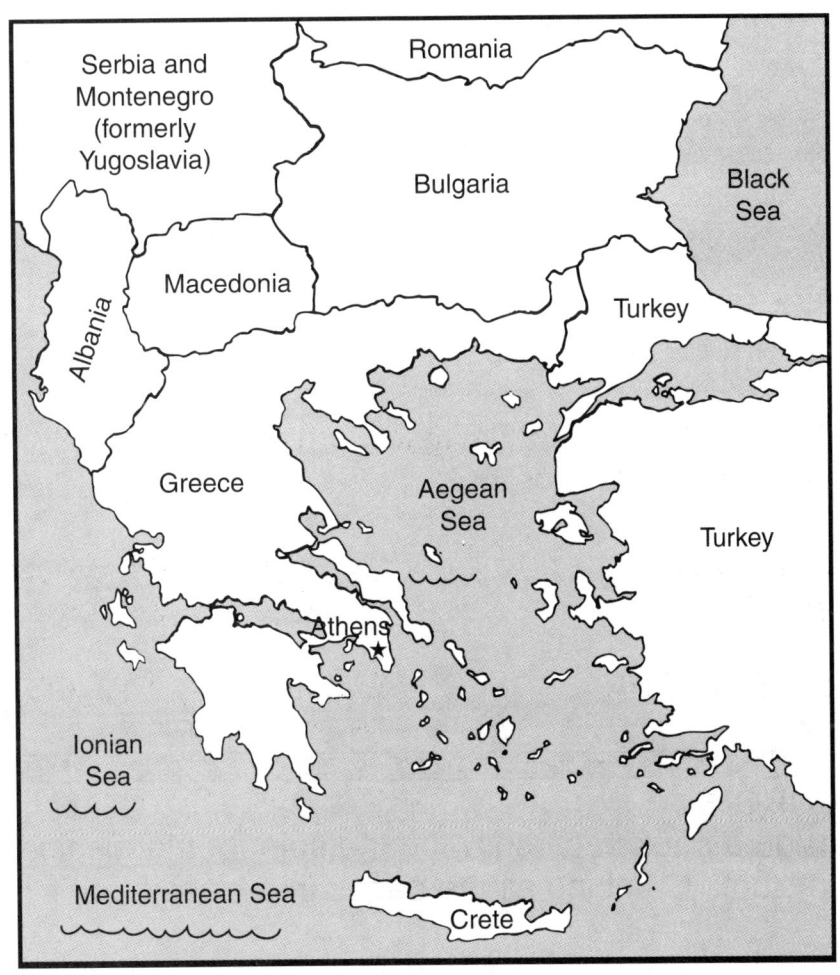

 # Olympic Spirit

Baron Pierre de Coubertin knew that the Olympic Games would bring together athletes from all over the world. He hoped they would become good friends. This is the spirit of the Olympic Games.

Who are your friends? _____

_____

What sports or games do you like to play together? _____

_____

Tell one way in which you are a good friend. _____

_____

Draw a picture of you and your friends playing together.

Extension: Design a book page showing the spirit of friendship. Write a story to explain your picture. Combine all the pages in a class book titled, **The Spirit of Friendship**.

Do Your Best

The Olympic athlete's creed states, "The most important thing in the Olympic Games is not to win but to take part, just as the most important thing in life is not the triumph but the struggle. The essential thing is not to have conquered but to have fought well."

This is a good lesson for life. You can always be proud of yourself if you work hard and do your best. Think about the things you do every day. Complete these sentences:

Yesterday I did my best _____.

Today I will do my best _____.

Tomorrow I will do my best _____.

CONGRATULATIONS

to

_____

For working hard at

_____

_____

_____ _____
Teacher's Signature   *Date*

 # Play Fair

All Olympic athletes make a promise to play fair. Here are the words in the oath they take:

In the name of all competitors, I promise that we shall take part in these Olympic Games, respecting and abiding by the rules which govern them, in the true spirit of sportsmanship, for the glory of the sport, and the honor of our teams.

Why is it important to follow the rules of a sport? _____

_____

Tell one way in which you follow rules in sports or games. _____

_____

Tell one way in which you follow rules in the classroom or at home. _____

_____

Write a promise that will help you follow rules in the classroom or at home.

I promise _____

_____

 # Olympic Village

The Athens Olympic Village will be home to 16,000 athletes and coaches from around the world. It has two parts, one with apartments where the athletes live and the other with shops and businesses. The village is the biggest housing project ever built in Greece.

The athletes will be able to rest in private apartments. When they have free time, they may visit nearby shops, dining halls, and entertainment centers. There will also be a church and a medical center. All athletes will have transportation to their events.

Draw an Olympic Village in the space below. Include all the buildings listed in the story.

The Olympic Village

Extension: Discuss how the Olympic Village is alike or different from the town or city in which you live.

 # Training Table

As many as six thousand meals will be served every hour at the Athens Olympic Village. Workers will plan and prepare meals for athletes using the same recipes and foods they eat in their home countries. All athletes need good nutrition in order to do their best.

Make a list of ten healthy foods:

_____   _____
_____   _____
_____   _____
_____   _____
_____   _____

Choose five foods to make a meal and draw that meal on the plate.

Extension: On the back of this paper, draw three healthy snacks for an athlete. Explain why you chose each one.

 # Venues

There are three main locations for the 2004 Olympic Games. They are the **Athens Olympic Sports Complex**, the **Hellinikon Olympic Complex**, and the **Faliron Olympic Coastal Zone Complex**. Each complex has more than one field or stadium where athletes will practice and compete.

* **The Athens Olympic Sports Complex** will host six sports: athletics (track and field), basketball, cycling (track), gymnastics, swimming, and tennis.

* **The Hellinikon Olympic Complex** will host five sports: badminton, baseball, softball, fencing, and hockey.

* **The Faliron Olympic Coastal Zone Complex** will host seven sports: basketball, beach volleyball, volleyball, boxing, handball, judo, and taekwondo.

Select one of the Olympic venues. Draw a picture in the space below of two of the featured sports that will be played there.

 # Olympic Logos

Summer Events

Cut out the Olympic Logos cards along the dotted lines. (You may want to laminate them for durability.) Use them in a variety of activities. Here are some ideas:

- Students can alphabetize the cards.
- Pairs of students can use the cards to play an Olympic version of "Go Fish" or "Concentration."
- Students can create different ways to sort the cards.
- Have the students place the cards face down in a pile. Working in pairs, have students take turns picking one card at a time. The student will share everything he or she knows about that sport. When finished, the partner can add any details that may have been left out.
- Use the cards as part of an Olympic-medals class chart. Place them on a bulletin board or large sheet of paper and record medal winners next to the corresponding sport.
- Let the students select a card to use as a visual story starter. Younger children can write three things they like about that sport and three things they don't like. Older students may want to create a fictional story about a child their age involved in that sport.
- Have your students create their own unique activity to share with the class.

Archery

Athletics

Badminton

Baseball

 # Olympic Logos *(cont.)*

Summer Events *(cont.)*

Basketball

Boxing

Canoeing/Kayaking

Cycling

Diving

Fencing

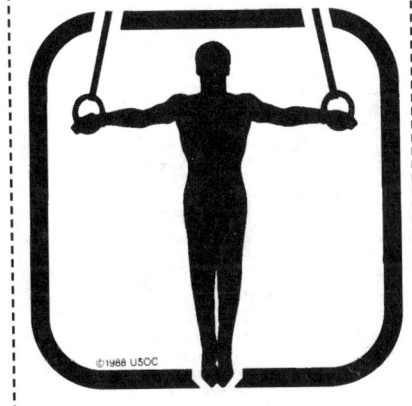
Gymnastics

Equestrian

Field Hockey

 # Olympic Logos *(cont.)*

Summer Events *(cont.)*

Judo

Modern Pentathlon

Rowing

Sailing

Shooting

Soccer

Softball

Swimming

Synchronized Swimming

 # Olympic Logos *(cont.)*

Summer Events *(cont.)*

Table Tennis

Taekwondo

Team Handball

Tennis

Triathlon

Volleyball

Water Polo

Weight Lifting

Wrestling

 # Sports to Sort

Cut out the cards below. Working with a partner, sort them into the following categories:

- Sports equipment
- Parts of an athlete's uniform
- Things that are used to strike a ball

Which category had the most cards? _____

Can you think of another category? _____

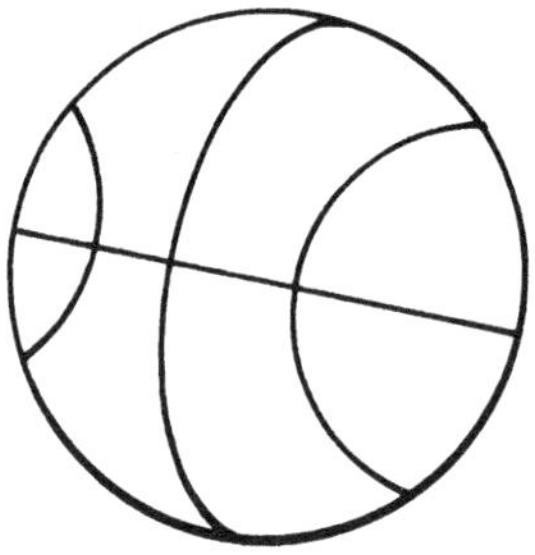

 # The Marathon

The marathon is a 26.2 mile (42 km) foot race. It is held on the last day of the Olympic Games. The race finishes at the same time as the closing ceremony so the runners come into a stadium full of cheering fans.

The first marathon was run in 490 B.C., by a Greek man named **Pheidippides**. He ran from the city of Marathon to Athens to report that the Greeks had defeated the Persian army. The marathon in the Athens 2004 Olympic Games will follow the same path, beginning at Marathon and ending in Athens at the Panathinaiko Stadium.

Another Greek man, **Spyridon Louis**, won the first Olympic marathon in 1896. He had no special training to be a runner. Today, runners practice every day in all kinds of weather. They wear light clothing and special shoes. Runners need to get plenty of sleep and eat well to do their best.

Working as a class, determine one or more locations that are approximately 26 miles from school. Discuss what you would see on a trip to each of those locations and what it would be like to walk (or run) that distance.

Extension: If your school has a track, try running around it. How many times around equals one mile? What about 26.2 miles? If there is no track, create your own! (Remember, 1 mile = 5,280 feet).

Track and Field Jeopardy

Read the clues. Complete each question by filling in the blank. Use the word bank at the bottom of the page for help.

Example: Races are run on this.

What is a _____ track _____ *?*

1. This is a 26.2 mile foot race.

   What is a _____ *?*

2. This race is run by a four-person team.

   What is a _____ *?*

3. In this sport, the athlete uses a long pole to jump over a high bar.

   What is the _____ *?*

4. In this sport, the athlete throws a small, metal ball.

   What is the _____ *?*

5. In this sport, the athlete throws a spear.

   What is the _____ *?*

6. This is the name of the shortest, fastest running event.

   What is the _____ *?*

7. There are ten events in this contest for men.

   What is the _____ *?*

8. There are seven events in this contest for women.

   What is the _____ *?*

Word Bank

| marathon | relay race | javelin throw | shot put |
| decathlon | heptathlon | pole vault | sprint or dash |

Note to Teacher: Fold under along the dotted lines before copying.

Answers: 1. marathon   2. relay race   3. pole vault   4. shot put
   5. javelin throw   6. sprint or dash   7. decathlon   8. heptathlon

 # Top Athlete

To complete this puzzle, begin at **Start**. Follow the arrow around the circle. Write every other letter—beginning with the letter "H"—and you will find two words that tell what it takes to be a winner.

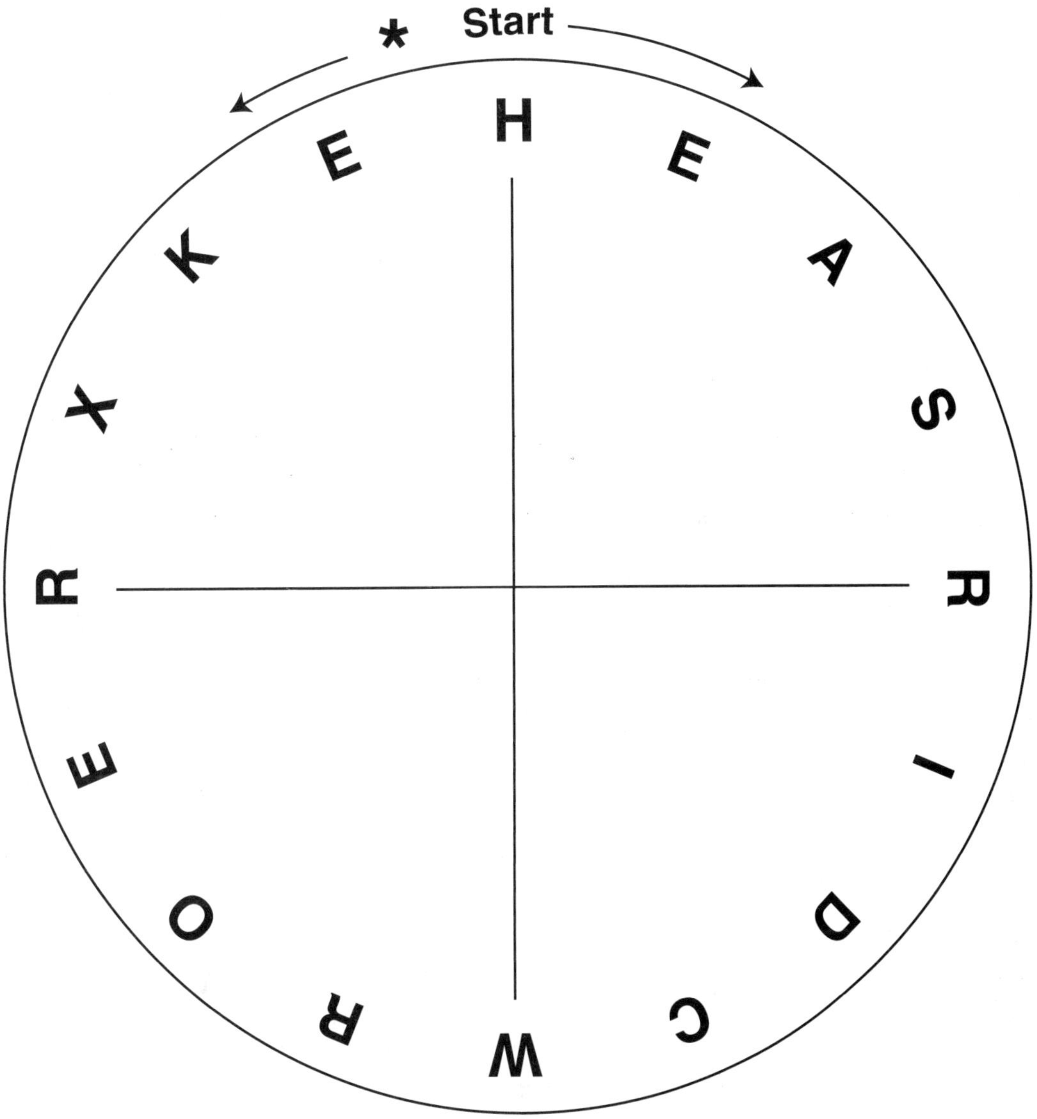

Bonus: Start at the star (*) and follow the arrow going in the opposite direction. Write every other letter, beginning with the letter "E." Find a word that tells something athletes do every day.

Note to Teacher: Fold under along the dotted lines before copying.
Answer: hard work
Bonus: exercise

 # Bend and Stretch

All athletes know the importance of warm-up exercises to prepare their bodies for action. See if you can match the exercises described on the left to the correct picture on the right. Then, try these bends and stretches for yourself! Remember to bend and stretch slowly.

_____ 1. Sit with the bottoms of your feet together. Press your knees to the floor.

_____ 2. Stand by the wall. Put your hands on it. Push off as if you are doing push-ups.

_____ 3. Lie on your stomach. Slowly lift your head and legs. Arch your back.

_____ 4. Lie on your back. Bend your knees. Put your hands behind your head. Sit up.

_____ 5. Squat like a frog with your fingers on the floor. Jump up high.

_____ 6. Put your hands flat on the wall. Take a step back. Look down. Keep your back flat.

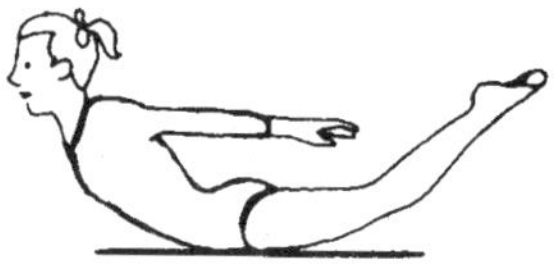

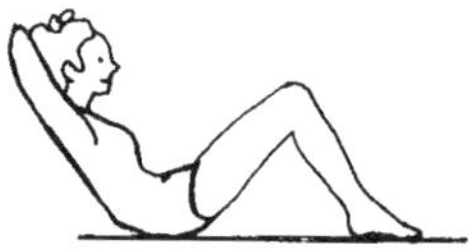

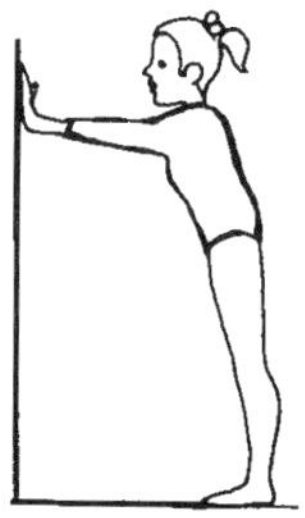

Note to Teacher: Fold under along the dotted lines before copying.

Answers: 1. C 2. E 3. A 4. D 5. F 6. B

United States Medal Winners

Teachers: You may wish to enlarge this chart and post it on your classroom wall or make individual copies for the students to work on independently.

Each morning, ask students to report on the United States medal winners from the previous day's events. Record the sport, the athlete's name, and medal information on the list. Make a yellow (gold), gray (silver), or brown (bronze) circle to show the winning medal.

Sport	Athlete's Name	Medal

Extension Activities:

- On another sheet of paper, have students make a graph showing how many of each of the medals (gold, silver, bronze) were won by the United States.

- In addition to keeping track of U.S. medals, let each student or group of students select a different country to track and report on, keeping a separate chart and medal count for that nation.

Making a Mascot

The Olympic Games mascot represents the host city and country in some way. Phevos and Athena, the mascots for the Athens 2004 Olympic Games, are brother and sister dolls that look like very old Greek toys. They are named after Greek gods.

Think about the city where you live or a city that you know well. What makes it a special place? Draw a mascot for the city.

The Flag and Emblem

Flag

Baron de Coubertin, father of the modern Olympic Games, used five rings to represent the continents of the world: North and South America (counted as one), Europe, Asia, Africa, and Australia. The rings are blue, yellow, black, green, and red because every flag in the world has one of those colors. The rings are linked because Baron de Coubertin hoped the athletes would become friends. The five colored rings on a white background became the Olympic flag in 1914. It is carried into the opening ceremony by athletes from each of the five continents.

Color the rings of the Olympic flag, as indicated.

Emblem

Each host city has an emblem that is different from the flag with five rings. It may show things to do or places to see in the city. There is a picture of a discus thrower on the emblem of the ancient Greek Olympic Games. He represents the strength and power of all athletes. The emblem for Athens, 2004, is a white olive-branch circle on a blue background.

Extension: Design an Olympic Games emblem showing things to do or see in your city.

 # Medals

Ancient Olympians won a crown made of olive leaves. Today, winners receive gold, silver, or bronze medals. Medals are about three inches (seven centimeters) across and have a picture of a Greek goddess on the front.

Complete the medal below by adding:

- the five Olympic Rings
- the words, "Athens, Greece"
- the year, "2004"

Color the medal yellow (gold), gray (silver), or light brown (bronze).

 # The Torch Relay

The torch for the Athens 2004 Olympic Games is made of wood from the olive tree and aluminum. It will be lit by the heat of the sun in Olympia, Greece. Runners will carry it to every continent in the world before it returns to Greece. In Athens, the torch will be used to light the flame at the opening of the Olympic Games. The torch relay is one way in which people all around the world can take part in the Olympic Games.

Color the torch below as indicated. Then, write a sentence telling one fact from the story on the lines.

1 = yellow
2 = orange
3 = black
4 = purple

Olympic Fact

 # Bibliography

Bauer, Larry. *Easy Olympics Sports Readers.* Teacher Created Materials, Inc., 1998.

Crowther, Robert. *Robert Crowther's Pop-Up Olympics: Amazing Facts and Record Breakers.* Candlewick Press, 1996. out of print, limited availability

Ditchfield, Christin. *Cycling, True Book Series.* Children's Press, 2000.

———. *Gymnastics, True Book Series.* Children's Press, 2000.

———. *Kayaking, Canoeing, and Yachting, True Book Series.* Children's Press, 2000.

———. *Swimming and Diving, True Book Series.* Children's Press, 2000.

———. *Wrestling, True Book Series.* Children's Press, 2000.

Fischer, David. *The Encyclopedia of the Summer Olympics.* Franklin Watts, Inc., 2003.

Hennessey, B.G. *Olympics!* Puffin Books, 2000

Holzschuher, Cynthia. *United States Olympic Committee's Curriculum Guide to the Olympic Games: The Olympic Dream.* Griffin Publishing/Teacher Created Materials, Inc., 2000.

Knotts, Bob. *Equestrian Events, True Book Series.* Children's Book Press, 2000.

———. *Martial Arts, True Book Series.* Children's Press, 2000.

———. *The Summer Olympics, True Book Series.* Children's Press, 2000.

———. *Track & Field, True Book Series.* Children's Press, 2000.

———. *Weightlifting, True Book Series.* Children's Press, 2000.

Kristy, Davida. *Coubertin's Olympics: How the Games Began.* Lerner Publishing, 2003.

Ledeboer, Suzanne. *Olympism: A Basic Guide to the History, Ideals, and Sports of the Olympic Movement.* Griffin Publishing, 2001.

Middleton, Hayden. *Great Olympic Moments.* Heinemann Library, 1999.

Osbourne, Mary Pope. *Hour of the Olympics.* Random House, 1998.

Oxlade, Chris. *Eyewitness: Olympics.* DK Publishing, 2000.

Ross, Stewart. *The Original Olympics.* Peter Bendrick Books, 1999.

Web Sites

- http://www.athens2004.com
- http://www.edgate.com/summergames/inactive/olympic_spirit/baron_pierre.html
- http://www.forthnet.gr/olympics/athens1896/
- http://www.greece-2004.com/athens_2004_olympic_games/
- http://www.sikids.com
- http://www.timeforkids.com
- http://www.worldalmanacforkids.com